T0065370

Diamonds in the Darkness

Stories of Faith and Inspiration during Difficult Times

Heather L. Smith

WESTBOW
P R E S S®
A DIVISION OF THOMAS NELSON
& ZONDERVAN

WestBow Press books may be ordered through booksellers or by contacting:

WestBow Press
A Division of Thomas Nelson & Zondervan
1663 Liberty Drive
Bloomington, IN 47403
www.westbowpress.com
844-714-3454

ISBN: 978-1-6642-0127-9 (sc)
ISBN: 978-1-6642-0129-3 (hc)
ISBN: 978-1-6642-0128-6 (e)

Library of Congress Control Number: 2020914698

Print information available on the last page.

WestBow Press rev. date: 9/23/2020

To

My cherished mother,

Julia C. Lee

All my love

Contents

Preface

Dearly Beloved,

You are deeply loved by God. You are His most precious creation. You are His child. You are His beloved!

There is no one like you. The Father designed you uniquely and gave you tremendous gifts that will achieve His great purposes and give your life deep significance.

God has a plan for your life, my friend. His purpose will bring deep meaning and satisfy the longings of your heart.

As you rejoice over His goodness, know that He is preparing you for something wonderful. The Father has plans that will give you a hope and a future (see Jeremiah 29:11).

God will provide for you. Cast all your anxiety on him because he cares for you (1 Peter 5:7). Rest in Him today for you are His beloved child.

God loves you!

A Glimpse of Heaven

Set your minds on things above,

not on earthly things.

For you died, and your life is now

hidden with Christ in God.

When Christ, who is your life,

appears, then you also will

appear with him in glory.

—Colossians 3:2–4

Dearly Beloved,

Not long ago, I attended a Christian concert with my

daughter and her best friend. The weather was dreary

and cold, but I was excited about the special evening that lay in front of us. It didn't matter that the concert was two hours away. I knew that we would be blessed!

We arrived early and looked around. People from all walks of life surrounded us. There were people in formal dress and individuals who dressed according to the cold weather, like me.

I went to my seat and observed the large audience. It looked like about one thousand people were there. The hall was filled with reserved persons; I thought it was strange that these people were here. They were quiet, talking softly to their neighbors. This was unlike Christian concerts I had attended where excitement filled the audience.

I waited with expectancy as we watched the renowned Christian artist, the choir of several hundred people, and a vast orchestra slowly take their places. The music was incredible, and I was captivated by the rich sounds of the orchestra. The choir was extraordinary; it sounded like the voices of thousands of angels.

Suddenly I was caught up in the glorious presence of God. Complete joy permeated the entire atmosphere. A thousand people, before quiet and reserved, were standing and singing at full volume, extending their hands upward toward Jesus.

Gone were the concerns and worries that had plagued me for months. I never wanted to go home again!

Dearly beloved, one day we will be in heaven, worshipping the Lord Jesus Christ. John said in his book of Revelation that His face was like the sun shining in all its brilliance (Revelation 1:16). And we will be with Him forever.

My friend, whenever you are alone and afraid, remember these words of Jesus: "In this world you will have trouble. But take heart! I have overcome the world" (John 16:33).

God loves you. He is for you. (See Romans 8:31.) If you don't know Jesus, please take a moment and ask Him into your heart. Tell Him that you are sorry for your sins and that you want to live with Him forever. Be encouraged today, and know that our King has your every care in His hands. (See 1 Peter 5:7.)

God loves you!

God Speaks

So is my word that goes out from
mouth: it will not return to me empty,
but will accomplish what I desire and
achieve the purpose for which I sent it.

—Isaiah 55:11

Dearly Beloved,

On a beautifully clear afternoon in early June, my
mother was sitting with my dad on their little back
deck. The sky overhead was a beautiful, cloudless
blue; not the smallest cloud could be seen. Clusters of
butterflies swarmed over the purple blooms of a nearby

butterfly bush, and the comforting drone of bees could be heard on the flowers.

Sadly, my dad had been stricken with Alzheimer's some years before, not just with Alzheimer's but with a rare type that caused him to yell incessantly and loudly during his every waking moment. So on this beautiful, cloudless afternoon, he was sitting in his deck chair and yelling at the top of his voice. From that clear blue sky, a sudden sharp crack of thunder crashed through the atmosphere. And my dad stopped yelling.

It was as though God had said to him, "Be still" (Psalm 46:10). And Dad heard Him and was still. For the rest of that beautiful afternoon, the greatest sense of peace stayed with us as we sat together on that little back deck.

Dad passed away at home on August 9, 2013, at the age of ninety-one. Today he is rejoicing in heaven with Jesus.

So take comfort, my friend, if you are going through

the valley of the shadow. Your Father is with you, and He will quiet your heart with His peace.

You are His precious child, and He loves you more than life. Please take His hand and allow Him to comfort you during the dark days. You will see His strong, silent love in marvelous ways. Be still, and wait on Him.

God loves you!

The Power of Prayer

Therefore I tell you, whatever you ask
for in prayer, believe that you have
received it, and it will be yours.

—Mark 11:24

Dearly Beloved,

Our Father delights in communicating with us. He cares for everything that concerns us. He wants to be in our lives and walk with us through the good times and the bad. He is our precious Father.

Over the years of living alone, I have come to rely completely on Him. I pray continually, particularly when I am in difficult situations and don't know what to do.

Two years ago, I got in my car and started to work. As I was driving down the road, I noticed a loud noise from under the hood. I decided to drive to the dealer instead of to work. The noise would not stop, and I had to drive about ten miles to my destination. Praying hard that God would keep me safe, I drove faster than usual. About two miles from the dealer, I smelled something burning. I didn't want to stop because I was afraid the car wouldn't start again. I prayed fervently that God would keep me safe and get me to the dealer before the car blew up.

The Father answered my prayers, and I pulled into the lot safely. The car, however, was not so fortunate. It would not start. The servicemen said it needed major repairs, too much to spend on a ten-year-old car. That was fine with me. I was thankful that God had kept me safe throughout the horrible ordeal.

That is the kind of God we serve. He wants to be involved in your life. Everything that matters to you matters to Him. He created you and knows your deepest heartaches and what brings you unspeakable joy.

If you don't know the Creator of your life, please take a moment, and ask Jesus to come into your heart. He wants you to be with Him forever.

God loves you!

4

Jesus Loves You

For God so loved the world that

he gave his one and only Son, that

whoever believes in him shall not

perish but have eternal life.

—John 3:16

Dearly Beloved,

In 2013 I lost my job. I loved working and had been at

this position for ten years. Two weeks later, I lost my

father. The tremendous loss took a toll on me physically,

spiritually, and mentally. I felt like my life was over.

Certainly I was getting older, so the prospects of a new

job were slim. Living alone, it was hard to know what to do. I sank into depression and believed my life was over. *Maybe,* I thought, *God doesn't need me anymore.*

It's easy to feel that way, isn't it, beloved? When our lives change for the worse, we wonder what we did wrong. I had a beautiful home in the woods, but it had a steep mortgage, and my pension was dwindling. It was hard to see into the future, and I forgot God's promise to never leave or forsake me.

Ultimately, I got sick from sadness and worry, and my energy plummeted. I had no desire to do anything but sit in my recliner and feel sorry for myself. My family was my only comfort. They loved me dearly, and I always enjoyed being with them.

A year went by, and I was still stuck in my recliner. I didn't have the stamina to clean the house. I tried to find a job, but nothing worked. My children were very concerned; they weren't used to their mother feeling so hopeless.

They suggested I look into volunteering. It would give me a chance to help others and get out of the house a few times a week. I visited Hanover County, where I live, and was eventually hired for two positions: one answering calls and the other updating databases. Over time, I began to feel better, like I was wanted and needed.

However, from not doing anything for a year and then suddenly volunteering several days a week, my body protested under the stress, and I got sick. That went on for another year, and I finally ended in the hospital, not sure if I would live. That day was a wake-up call for me.

I didn't know how much time I had on this earth, but I did know I wanted to make a difference with the time I had left. I lay on my bed at night, and the Father held me in His arms. A picture in my den of Jesus holding a young man up comforted me. I knew Jesus was also holding me up. I lay in the bed and prayed for my family, for other families, for unborn children, and for children all over the world who needed love, food, clothing, and care. I prayed for our nation to come back to God. I prayed for the lost who were deceived.

About three weeks later, I started to walk a little. It helped, and I determined to walk a little every day. And I read my Bible at night, letting the verses of God's comfort and compassion wash over my exhausted mind.

Slowly and surely, I began to be myself again. I had secluded myself from life for such a long time, and now I can begin again, as long as Jesus holds me up.

Dearly beloved, Jesus loves you so much. You are His cherished child! You may be going through a terrible time and cannot see any end in sight. You have hung on as long as you could, but nothing is happening. You may have no home, no job, and no income, no one who can help you. You may have experienced unbearable loss. You may be sick or lonely and depressed, and you wonder why God hasn't taken you home. You are so tired and don't feel like walking another step.

My beloved, Jesus is walking with you through the fire: "When you pass through the waters, I will be with you; and when you pass through the rivers, they will not sweep over you. When you walk through the fire, you will not be burned; the flames will not set you ablaze" (Isaiah 43:2). He knows where He is taking you—a place of wonder where you will be able to share His faithfulness during the hard times. He is shaping your life into a magnificent story that will bring the Father glory and touch the lives of thousands with His incredible love. He loves you, dear friend, and He has boundless plans for your life. Allow Him to walk with you. This difficult journey will be over soon, and you will see that it was worth it to bring the Father the highest praise.

God loves you!

Trust Him

In all your ways acknowledge him, and
he will make your paths straight.

—Proverbs 3:6

Dearly Beloved,

How are you today? Are you happy and celebrating life, rejoicing in God's wonderful blessings, or are you experiencing overwhelming sadness and going through a difficult time? If it is the latter, my dear, may I share some words of comfort? God sees your pain. The precious One knows where you are, my beloved. He loves you very much. You are His treasured child. The

Father is your precious Daddy. He will take care of you. Lean on Him, and rest in His strong arms of love. Listen to His heartbeat and sweet whispers of love.

My dear friend, the Father sees your sorrow. Cast all your anxiety on him because he cares for you (1 Peter 5:7). Cling to Him as you travel through the wilderness. Look for His expressions of love for <u>you alone</u> every day. The King of Kings and Lord of Lords will lead you safely through the abyss. He will bring hope into your heart as He leads you out of the darkness and into the sunshine.

There are times of laughter and rejoicing that are waiting for you, my beloved. For now, rest in Him, and know that your Father dearly loves you!

Total Dependence

In my distress I called to the Lord;

I cried to my God for help.

From his temple he heard my voice; my

cry came before him, into his ears

—Psalm 18:6

Dearly Beloved,

God is my strength, my Redeemer, and my provider. He is everything to me. I depend totally on Him for every breath I take and every need. Without Him, I can do nothing. He is my Source. God is my Father; I am His beloved child.

Sometime ago I became extremely ill. My head throbbed, and nothing eased the pain.

Sleep evaded me for days. I wasn't able to work, visit my family, clean my home, or anything.

I finally went to the doctor. He prescribed a medication we both hoped would work. The pain subsided at night, when all of the lights were out, but returned in the morning. The hours dragged by, and misery consumed me.

Not being around anyone, the devil easily entered my mind. "God doesn't love you anymore," he said. "He has finished with you."

It was easy to believe the lies. I truly believed my life was over, and God had no more plans for me. Living alone with a thirty-year mortgage, finances shrinking, long lonely nights, and now I was sick.

I knew I needed to talk to God, so every night as I lay down, I said, "The Lord is my shepherd, I shall not be in want" (Psalm 23:1). And He answered. In the depth of my anguish, God reminded me of my many blessings: a beautiful home close to my family, in the woods, a good car, relatively good health, an incredible church where I was loved by many, and my family and friends who adored me.

I continued to focus on my blessings, like Philippians 4:8 reminds us, and even though my pain continued, I recognized God's tremendous blessings on my life, and I worshipped the King of Kings and the Lord of Lords.

Jesus is my Redeemer; my Savior; my provider; the author and finisher of my faith; my Comforter; my peace; my soon-coming King; my counselor; my rescuer; the Good Shepherd; my judge; the lily of the valley; the Lamb without spot or blemish; the rose of Sharon; a friend who is closer than a brother; the blessed hope; the Messiah; the Bread of Life; the Light of the World; the door; the way, the truth, and the life; the true vine; the resurrection; God in the flesh; Emanuel.

I had to rely on Him for everything just to get

through the day. From finding a parking space near a basket at the crowded grocery store, saying a prayer that someone would come and help me buy some groceries or help me to the car with my packages. I said unspoken prayers that He would help me find things in my home, help me not to fall, and to give me the strength to take one more step. He is always faithful, and I take great comfort in knowing that God hears my every cry and answers my prayers.

God is sovereign. I am in His hands until He calls me home!

My precious friend, even though you may be going through desperate times, He will carry you through and one day bring laughter and joy into your heart.

He will take great delight in you, he will quiet you with his love, he will rejoice over you with singing (Zephaniah 3:17).

God loves you!

Courage

Be strong and courageous. Do not be

terrified; do not be discouraged,

for the Lord your God will be

with you wherever you go.

—Joshua 1:9

Dearly Beloved,

God told Joshua to be of great courage when Joshua

was preparing to cross over to the Promised Land.

Many times He does the same with us, tells us to

be courageous whether we are going on a mission trip,

talking to an unsaved neighbor, volunteering, or visiting

the sick. We are His hands and His feet, so we need to discern His perfect will for our lives.

Sometimes we say no to God. The task He has for us may be too hard. The Bible tells great stories of people who said no to God. However, God has no plan B; we are it. So even though Moses, Jonah, and a lot of others turned their backs on God, it was only for a short time.

How would you like to be in a whale's body for three days? Jonah was in the whale's belly for three days and three nights (see Jonah 1:17).

When we reach rock bottom, God shows up. He promises to only allow those things that we can handle. And God is faithful; he will not let you be tempted beyond what you can bear (1 Corinthians 10:13).

So beloved, when God asks you to do something, rejoice for you are serving the Creator of the universe, and He chose you.

God loves you!

The Arms of Jesus

Cast all your anxiety on him

because he cares for you

—1 Peter 5:7

Dearly Beloved,

Life can be hard. Jobs are lost, businesses fold, loved ones get sick, homes go into foreclosure, and we lose hope. Hope that tomorrow will be better. Despondency, depression, and hopelessness knock us down flat.

Dear friend, look up! There is a Savior. His name is Jesus. He is our deliverer. He is sovereign. He knows all things before they happen. If you have accepted

Him into your heart, you belong to Him forever. He is holding you in His strong arms of love, where you are safe and warm.

My friend, you have the privilege of calling your Father "Daddy" (see Romans 8:15). He loves you dearly. He will supply <u>all</u> your needs (see Philippians 4:19).

Spend time in His precious Word. He who dwells in the shelter of the Most High will rest in the shadow of the Almighty. I will say of the Lord, "He is my refuge and my fortress, my God, in whom I trust" (Psalm 91:1–2).

Stay close to Jesus, dearly beloved. He has your every care in His hand (see 1 Peter 5:7).

God loves you!

The Christmas Season

Today in the town of David a Savior has
been born to you; he is Christ the Lord.

—Luke 2:11

Come to me, all you who are weary
and burdened, and I will give you rest.

—Matthew 11:28

Dearly Beloved,

Christmas is a time of celebration of the birth of our
precious Savior, Jesus Christ. Smells of freshly cut trees,
baked cinnamon cookies, brightly wrapped presents,

and hot cocoa fill our thoughts with blissful delight. Friends we may not have seen in years call or send cards to let us know they are thinking of us. Buying gifts is exciting during this time of the year. People are kinder than ever and go out of their way to express joyous wishes. Church bells ring louder, and the aisles are filled with people holding candles and softly singing Christmas carols.

For many people, however, Christmas is a painful time. Loved ones have passed, finances are strained, jobs are lost, and health problems are taking a tremendous toll. All they want are the holidays to be over.

You may be one of these people. My dear friend, the Lord understands so well the hurt and pain you are experiencing. As you walk through the wilderness, my beloved, you will discover how much the Lord Jesus Christ loves you. He is tenderly watching over you to make sure you are all right.

As you begin to depend on the heavenly Father to

provide your every need, you will encounter His daily expressions of love. It is in the darkness where you see His strong, silent love. You will discover, my dear, He is preparing you for something wonderful, and in a little while, He will replace all your hurt with His incredible joy!

When my thirty-year marriage ended, the holidays brought back so many memories that it took a tremendous toll on me. There had been lots of parties and fun times during the season. Now they were over.

However, through my grief and sorrow, I discovered that Christmas is not simply a fun time but a time to reach out to other hurting people. I was not up to giving gifts, but I was able to send Christmas cards to lonely people like myself. God is faithful. He put so many friends and loved ones in my heart who needed a word of hope. On Christmas Eve I was still stuffing mailboxes with my cards of encouragement.

I found that in sharing my life with others, the hurt

and pain began to dissipate. Reaching out to other hurting people brought healing to my heart.

I started new traditions. I decided not to decorate for the holidays but spend Christmas with my daughter and her husband for a few days. Getting away from home and memories was the best way to celebrate Christmas. I still do that, and the years of attending the sweet Christmas Eve service in my children's little country church and watching my grandchildren open their presents on Christmas morning have been tremendous blessings.

God will take you through this difficult time. He loves you. You are His precious child. So look for Him to show up for you during Christmas. He is always faithful.

God loves you!

His Majesty

Yours, O Lord, is the greatness

and the power and the glory

and the majesty and the splendor, for

everything in heaven and earth is yours.

Yours, O Lord, is the kingdom;

you are exalted as head over all.

—1 Chronicles 29:11

Who among the gods is like you, O Lord?

Who is like you— majestic in holiness,

awesome in glory, working wonders?

—Exodus 15:11

O Lord, our Lord, how majestic

is your name in all the earth!

—Psalm 8:1

It is good to praise the Lord and

make music to your name, O Most

High, to proclaim your love in the

morning and your faithfulness at

night, to the music of the ten-stringed

lyre and the melody of the harp.

—Psalm 92:1–3

Dearly Beloved,

The majesty of God! Who can comprehend it? He is
everywhere. The whole earth is celebrating the majesty
and glory of the King of Kings and Lord of Lords in
breathtaking splendor and magnificent beauty.

As a boy, David spent most of his time in the pastures,
tending the sheep. And he marveled at the magnificence
of God day and night as he slept under the vast heavens,

protecting his sheep and writing psalms of praise and thanksgiving. God loved him for David was a man after God's own heart (see Acts 13:22).

Paul said, "for since the creation of the world God's invisible qualities—his eternal power and divine nature—have been clearly seen, being understood from what has been made, so that men are without excuse" (Romans 1:20).

The world is extraordinary. Look up and gaze in wonder at the billions of stars shining in the heavens. Take time to appreciate the sweet-smelling rain falling gently on the earth, and enjoy a magnificent rainbow following a thunderstorm. And thank God you are alive. Watch a newborn deer trotting across the meadows with his mother beside him, or gaze at the roaring of the magnificent waves at the beach. Wake up to a glorious sunrise, and give thanks to your Father who made it! Visit a zoo and wonder at a loving God who made so many extraordinary creatures. Even a solitary walk down a quiet road can lead you to worship His majesty.

By drawing close to nature, we fall more in love with our Father, who made it and gave us charge to take care of it (see Genesis 1:28).

Dearly beloved, take some time today, and gaze at His marvelous creation. You will truly be blessed.

God loves you!

Diamonds in the Darkness

Do everything without

complaining or arguing,

so that you may become

blameless and pure,

children of God without fault in a

crooked and depraved generation,

in which you shine like stars in the

universe as you hold out the word

of life …

—Philippians 2:14–16

Dearly Beloved,

"God is good; life is hard," my pastor told me in a letter some time ago, when I unexpectedly lost my job. The odds of finding another were slim since I was getting older. Sometimes it's hard to go on, to face another day with all of its trials and challenges, wondering if I can possibly find the courage to endure when all hope seems to be gone.

Jesus said, "In this world you will have trouble. But take heart! I have overcome the world" (John 16:33).

Dear friend, this world is not our home. We belong to Jesus. One day we will live forever with Him—no more sorrow, no more pain. In the meantime, He will provide, He will comfort, He will make a way when all hope is gone. He loves you, and He has a tremendous plan for your life. In this sad and broken world, we are called to be children of light so we may shine for Him as we hold out the Word of life, and share God's love with lost and hurting people.

Yet, O Lord, you are our Father. We are the clay, you are the potter; we are all the work of your hand (Isaiah 64:8). The trials we go through are designed to mold us into the image of the Son.

God determines exactly how to fashion a beautiful piece of crystal from a charred broken bowl or a classical violin with an old chiseled saw. This task is left completely to Him, our Creator. He knows exactly what is needed.

As we minister to others, His glory permeates from within our brokenness. We may not be aware of it, dearly beloved, but the world sees it and many hunger for more. We have the unprecedented opportunity to spread His fragrance around those we come into contact with, sometimes without saying a word.

But thanks be to God, who always leads us in triumphal procession in Christ and through us spreads everywhere the fragrance of the knowledge of him. For we are to God the aroma of Christ among those who are being saved and those who are perishing. To the one we are the smell of death; to the other, the fragrance of life (2 Corinthians 2:14–16).

So rejoice, my beloved, for the King has given you a precious gift to share and bless others, and you in turn will see many brought into the kingdom.

God loves you!

My Child

How great is the love the Father has
lavished on us, that we should be called
children of God! And that is what we are!

—1 John 3:1

Dearly Beloved,

You are deeply loved by the Father. He created you in His
image and blessed you to be fruitful and multiply. You
were designed to rule over the fish in the sea and the birds
in the sky and over every living creature that moves on
the ground. He created you and me to have a relationship

with Him. In the beginning, He met Adam and Eve in the garden in the cool of the day (see Genesis 3:8).

Even after they sinned and were expelled from the garden, the Father showed them mercy by providing clothes for them to wear and food for them to eat. He blessed them with children of their own.

That is the God who loves us. Even when we walk away from Him, the Father continually calls us back to Himself. Even the angels in heaven rejoice when a sinner returns to the fold (see Luke 15:10).

We are His precious children, and He is eagerly anticipating the day that His children will be reunited with Him. Dearly beloved, stay close to the Father; He will prove Himself faithful. He adores you; there is nothing you can do that will take away His love for you (see Romans 8:35–39). Take time today to spend with your Daddy. Talk to Him about the burdens on your heart. Let Him wash away those precious tears and hold you in His strong arms of love.

God loves you!

Speak Life

The tongue has the power

of life and death,

and those who love it will eat its fruit.

—Proverbs 18:21

Pleasant words are a honeycomb, sweet

to the soul and healing to the bones.

—Proverbs 16:24

A gentle answer turns away wrath,

but a harsh word stirs up anger.

—Proverbs 15:1

A word aptly spoken is like apples

of gold in settings of silver.

—Proverbs 25:11

Dearly Beloved,

Every day we wake up we have the tremendous opportunity to be a blessing to others and to bring glory to the Father. Our words, dear friend, are deeply significant to those we speak to. When we speak softly words of love and encouragement, we speak life into another's heart. We give someone courage to keep going, to fight the good fight, to be kind to their families, to love their neighbors, and to carry the blessing forward. Our words and our hearts are in one harmony as we become more in love with Jesus. It's like Christmas every day of the year. Have you noticed? During the Holy Season, every word is a little kinder, a little softer, and we forgive people quicker.

It's one of the kindest things we can ever do for

humanity. Speak softly and love strongly. Try it tomorrow. Vow not to say one unkind word to anyone, no matter the situation, and watch what happens. You will be astonished at how quickly your words will affect someone's attitude. That person, in turn, will carry the torch of kindness to the next person. Our words are contagious. If we speak words of courage, faith, and love, it will be like a pebble being thrown into the sea, skipping to the next wave, changing it, and moving to the next wave.

Every human being on the planet has the intrinsic desire to love and to be loved. As they are drawn by the Holy Spirit, you, dearly beloved, will have the distinct opportunity to share what the King of Kings and Lord of Lords has done for you (see Revelation 12:11).

My precious friend, please spend time with the Creator. He will fill your heart to overflowing gratitude so that blessing others is a natural occurrence. And people will be drawn to the light within you, the Lord Jesus Himself. You, in turn, will be richly blessed and bring much pleasure to your Father in heaven.

God loves you!

Surprises

Taste and see that the Lord
is good; blessed is the man
who takes refuge in him.

—Psalm 34:8

Dearly Beloved,

I am always amazed when God shows up. I am not sure why. I love Him dearly, I pray for lonely, hurting people, I go to church and volunteer, but I mostly stay in my own little world.

Some time ago, the Father laid on my heart the need to declutter my garage. I had thirty years' worth of stuff. It was time to purge. Deciding to rent a shredder machine for the day, I went into the garage and glanced through the boxes of papers that needed to be demolished. I sifted through the boxes, pulling out snapshots of long ago, old coins, and treasured cards. I found three handmade love notes from a dear friend. Twenty years ago we were giving them away to people who need encouragement. Sweet pink and purple hearts with ribbons and sequins all over them saying, "Jesus loves you so very much." Inside the card said, "And so do we!"

I spent some time looking at them; they were so dear. Little did I know that the designer of those cards was at home frantically searching for one of those cherished cards for me! When I saw her the next day at church, she told me of her quest.

"You're too late," I told her. "God beat you to it." I gave her a picture of her artwork that had touched the lives of many people!

God loves to surprise us! Last Friday night, I attended a high school basketball game with my beautiful daughter. We were going to watch my granddaughter coach the cheerleaders. The night was cold, but we were really excited about watching Samantha at work. She had cheered herself for years, and now we were going to see my granddaughter coach her team. She still seemed like a little girl to me! In fact, toward the end of the game, she and her assistant were both cheering with the high school cheerleaders. It was a great night.

The girls' basketball teams were in full form too. The teams were evenly matched, and when one side scored, so did the other. It was a close game. So close, in fact, that the game went into overtime three times! My granddaughter said we couldn't come anymore. They had to stay for a second game.

When we first arrived in the gymnasium, a lady flew up behind me and yelled, "Are you Heather?" she asked. "Yes," I reluctantly answered. I didn't recognize her, and years of living alone have made me cautious.

"I am Sharon!" she cried. I looked closer and was amazed to see that she was my friend from long ago, over twenty-five years ago!

She readily left her family sitting at the other end of the gymnasium so she could sit with me and catch up. It was so much fun that we didn't even notice the kids sitting all around us. We were too busy getting reacquainted. Time stood still, and the game was all but forgotten. Sharon and I had been so close at one time, and I thought of her often. I even thought of sending her a Christmas card at my mother's insistence (she gave me the card), but I never did.

How did I know that God had planned something so much more wonderful than a Christmas card. He decided it was time for us to see each other face-to-face! As the game progressed, I got a chance to meet the rest of Sharon's family. They remembered me, and it was so wonderful renewing friendships. We laughed and hugged each other; it was like old times.

Beloved, that's what it is going to be like in heaven. A big party! Seeing friends from our past, present, and future. Won't that be glorious? Completely restored, fully loved, and fully able to see our beloved Father and the Lord Jesus Christ. My heart beats with excitement just thinking about it.

Dearly beloved, if you have lost contact with a dear friend today, put your trust in Christ. He knows where your friend is. And He is able to reinstate that relationship. That's what our Lord does best.

God loves you!

Unspeakable Joy

The Lord your God is with

you, he is mighty to save.

He will take great delight in you,

he will quiet you with his love,

he will rejoice over you with singing.

—Zephaniah 3:17

You have made known to

me the path of life;

You will fill me with joy in your presence,

with external pleasures

at your right hand.

—Psalm 16:11

Dearly Beloved,

There is no greater joy than spending time in the Father's presence. A quiet place that you have set aside for the Father to visit. A sweet place of quiet rest and perfect peace. Like a spring rain falling gently on tulips and daffodils in the early morning hour. When you walk through the door, the problems and hurts of the day are left behind. God is there in that little room waiting for you. The Father will anxiously be waiting for you, my dear. He looks forward to those special times of communion even more than you do.

As you sit patiently, silence permeates the atmosphere. You are in no hurry because God is there.

The glory of God begins to penetrate the room. Time ceases. There is just the Father and you. Take as long as you like; your God is in no hurry. And the longer you stay, the more you will change.

Spirit speaks to Spirit. You feel His love as it pours all over you; you breathe His presence. And the stresses of the day disappear as He holds you in His loving arms. You desire nothing but Him. Sometimes when you stay longer than usual, the walls and ceiling radiate a heavenly light, and a sweet holiness permeates the room. You feel like you could touch Him then. And you are reluctant to leave His arms of love. Tell Him everything—all your hopes for the future, your frustrations of the present, and the disappointments of the past. And He patiently listens and puts His arms around you. He comforts you with His presence. God gives you strength to face another day. Sometimes He may put a word in your heart or bring a person in mind to pray for. On other occasions it is just a time for you and Him alone. They are the best times.

As you seek Him regularly, your moments with Him will become rapturous delight. You will look forward to those times with great anticipation. And you will give your Father great pleasure.

In those quiet moments with Him, your Father will make you feel like you are the only person in the universe. That you are all who matters, just you alone. He loves you so much, my dear. You are His beloved. How great is the love the Father has lavished on us, that we should be called children of God (1 John 3:1).

My friend, let me invite you to spend time tonight with the Lord. He is eagerly waiting for you.

God loves you!

A Pure Heart

Create in me a pure heart, O God,

and renew a steadfast spirit within me.

Do not cast me from your presence

or take your Holy Spirit from me.

Restore to me the joy of your

salvation and grant me a willing

spirit, to sustain me.

—Psalm 51:10–12

Dearly Beloved,

It is a brand-new year! A time to let go of the past and commit to the present. A time to renew our faith and love to the Father. A time to leave the things we used to love and cling to righteousness. It's time to grow into the image of the Son! Pleasures that used to make you happy now no longer have any hold on you. Ignore those things that you used to do, and focus on the One who gave you life. For you were made for so much more.

You are the precious child of the Most High God, and He wants to take you up into the mountaintops to fall in love with Him all over again and to bring His glorious love to those left behind. His glory will be on your face, and it will be shared with a lost world. Stay close to God, my beloved. This is your time to bring praise to the Son and glory to God.

God loves you!

Learning to Rest

My Presence will go with you,

and I will give you rest.

—Exodus 33:14

Come to me, all you who are weary

and burdened, and I will give you rest.

—Matthew 11:28

Dearly Beloved,

Learning to rest requires focusing on God's faithfulness

of the past, what He has brought you through,

meditating on His glorious promises, and watching Him work on your behalf. Simply put, it means to trust.

The winter storm of 2016 tested my ability to rest in His strong arms of love without fear. Up to a foot of snow was expected to fall in the region over the weekend. Living alone is difficult, and a foot of snow was enough to terrify me. Living in the woods has tremendous advantages, but the long narrow driveway was difficult to manage even in good weather. Adding a foot of snow to the mix was like putting my life at risk. I opted for staying home until I was rescued. I focused on God and ignored the wintery blasts hurtling at my windows. Going to bed seemed liked a good idea also. The car had long since been buried by the wintery mix.

When I awoke, I was surprised that the lights were still on. God was still on the throne! Even though we had a foot of snow on the ground, I was warm, safe, and dry. I prayed earnestly for those who might not be.

Resting in God has not always been easy for me.

During a hurricane ten years earlier, I panicked and started packing, grabbing all my valuables, and getting ready to drive to my son's home in the middle of the howling winds. Eventually, the winds subsided; God had kept me safe.

Now, however, I am learning a new kind of rest, the rest that is described in Hebrews. Knowing that He has my entire future in His hands reassures me that the Father is always faithful and will carefully take care of His beloved. It means trusting the Creator.

Dearly beloved, the Father knows your needs before you ask. He created you and has wonderful plans for your life. If you don't know Him, please take a moment and ask the Lord Jesus Christ into your heart. You will never be sorry! He will comfort you during your darkest hour, restore your soul to new heights, provide for your daily needs, and bless you with His glorious presence.

As I looked out at the windows covered in ice and

snow, it was still snowing with no indication of stopping soon. But I knew that God was on the throne and knew exactly where His child was.

He knows where you are too, my friend.

Dear friend, keep looking up to your Father. He loves you and will keep you safe by His side for you are His beloved child.

God loves you!

A Changed Heart

I will give them an undivided heart

and put a new spirit in them;

I will remove from them their heart of

stone and give them a heart of flesh.

—Ezekiel 11:19

Dearly Beloved,

Many years ago, one of my dearest friends took me to a weekend seminar on the work of the Holy Spirit. I didn't know much about Him, but I did know my friend loved Jesus. Excitedly, I had my car checked out and packed my suitcase for the journey.

We had such a wonderful time talking about God that it only seemed like a few minutes before we arrived at the beautiful venue. We checked into a lovely hotel. There were people from all over the country, all overjoyed to be at the seminar. I felt like we were home. Everyone was family even though we had never met.

Hardly had we registered when a young man joined us. He had come alone and had no problem attaching himself to my friend and me. We saw him at breakfast, lunch, and supper. As we shared our stories, the young man eagerly told us about his incredible life. He had begun a career in drugs, dealing and using them for a long time, never knowing the love of Christ. One day his lifestyle suddenly ended, and he was thrown into prison, where he was scheduled to spend forty years behind bars.

There he was, alone and afraid. The years of jail

time ahead plunged him into deep despair. He had no hope for a future since he was already into his thirties.

One day, alone with his thoughts, he started to pray. It was his first time. "Father," he prayed, "if you get me out of here, I will serve you all the days of my life."

God hears your prayers, precious friend. Whether you are on the mountaintop or deep in the valley, He is always with you (see Psalm 139:8), and He will answer for your Daddy loves you.

The story ended victoriously. God heard my friend's desperate prayer, and a short time later he was released! He told us later that he looked at the person he used to be and wondered, *Who was that man?*

The story didn't end there, however. Sunday afternoon came, and I stepped into the ladies' room while my two friends enjoyed our last meal together. I looked in the mirror and prayed aloud, "Father, the seminar was good, but I didn't see any signs and wonders."

Immediately the Holy Spirit spoke to my heart. "There has been a sign and wonder following you around for three days. There is no greater sign and wonder than a changed heart!"

Jesus said, "it is easier for a camel to go through the eye of a needle than for a rich man to enter the kingdom of God." Those who heard this asked, "Who then who can be saved?" Jesus replied, "What is impossible with men is possible with God" (Luke 18:25–27).

Precious friend, keep praying for your unsaved friends and loved ones. And know that the Creator of the universe is listening and will answer.

God loves you!

The Mercy of God

Surely goodness and love will follow
me all the days of my life, and I will
dwell in the house of the Lord forever.

—Psalm 23:6

Dearly Beloved,

Sometimes it's hard to see God's love for us. When we
are unexpectedly knocked over by the trials of life, we
are unable to comprehend His eternal faithfulness. For
me it was giving up my job, my home, and going into
the hospital for weeks. Any of these hardships can be
devastating, but to experience all three at the same time

was overwhelming. At the age of seventy-five, I thought I would never recover and began to doubt the love of the Lord.

That's when the devil came in and shook my faith with his falsehoods. "You are finished. God doesn't love you anymore. What is there left on this earth for you to do? There is nothing for you anymore. All your hopes and dreams have been shattered. Your life is over," he whispered in my ear.

It's so easy when you have lost everything to give up all hope for a better tomorrow. You begin to fall into a black hole of despair. That's where I was, dearly beloved, broken and discouraged. Life no longer had meaning.

My friends reached out to me, but I didn't want to talk to anyone. The only people I allowed into my pain were my children. They were distressed at the sorrow and hopelessness that wrapped around me like a thick, tight glove. I didn't want to listen to Christian music, had no desire to read God's precious Word, and found it almost impossible to pray.

God wasn't ready to give up on me, however. One afternoon while in the hospital, a man walked in and asked if he could sit and pray with me. I said, "No, I'm good." I just wanted him to go away. Undeterred, he sat down and began to talk. He was a Christian and asked about my faith and the church I attended. I told him about the church I belonged to but hadn't been there in three years. I loved the people there but couldn't bear for them to see me in my current state. I was shocked to find out that the young man was a member of the same church. He said he would get in touch with the leadership and let them know I was in the hospital. I asked him not to, but he appeared not to hear me. He prayed with me and then left. I hoped he wouldn't tell my church family that I was sick.

Not long afterwards, I received a call. It was one of my friends and a staff member from my church. We talked a while, and she asked me to get in touch with her if I was still in the hospital the following Monday. I was still there but didn't call. I just wasn't up to it. That evening, however, my pastor, his wife, and a close friend walked in. I was shocked. They comforted and prayed over me. I was stilled loved and important to them even though I had not attended church in three years.

A few days later, another group from my church visited me. They brought little gifts of love, and we spent several minutes in prayer and fellowship. My friends encouraged me and gave me hope for the future.

I spent the next few weeks in and out of hospitals. It seemed to be one thing after another. When I went home, I was exhausted and thought I would never get well. An unexpected surgery left me weak and helpless. I depended on my children for everything as I clung to my walker to move even a few feet. My daughter took me to endless doctors' appointments, pushing me everywhere in a wheelchair. She and my son checked on me regularly. My grandchildren, Tabitha and Jimmy, were always available to help their granny in need.

In the midst of my distress, God continued to show up. A prescription costing $200 was suddenly reduced to $100. When the heat pump broke during the hottest day of the year, the maintenance man promptly came over and installed a brand-new temporary window air-conditioning unit.

The sun woke me very early one morning, and I found it difficult to go back to sleep. My kind daughter-in-law immediately went out and bought me black-out curtains. And I received good news from one of my doctors and was thrilled to know I didn't have to see him for six months.

Each time I was discouraged, God sent me unexpected phone texts from friends who prayed for me. I was always amazed at the timeliness of the comforting words; they came just when I needed them.

One day on route to surgery, I was surprised to receive an encouraging text from a friend who did not know about the operation.

During my suffering, my first great-grandson was born to my grandson, Cory and his beautiful wife, Stevie. What a joyful occasion for my entire family! A darling little boy we had been praying for came at the right time, a time when we all needed some wonderful news! Weighing in at nine pounds and two ounces, this adorable child was loved and celebrated by the whole family. A new generation had come into our lives.

After two months of being down and out, I went on the internet and looked for my church. I was thrilled to find that the sermons were available online. I started looking at them and decided it was time to go back to church. My thoughtful daughter took me to the morning service.

Oh, dear friend, God makes a way when all hope is gone. He cares for you, precious friend, so very much.

When you are going through hard times, He is right there. He sees your sorrow. He knows all about it. He understands because He has been there Himself. He has walked in your shoes. Lean on Him and know that the great Comforter is by your side.

God loves you!

Restoration

Praise be to the God and Father

of our Lord Jesus Christ,

the Father of compassion and

the God of all comfort,

who comforts us in all our troubles,

so that we can comfort those

in any trouble with the comfort

we ourselves receive from God.

—2 Corinthians 1:3–4

Dearly Beloved,

When we trust in Christ, we have a hope that can never leave us. He promises to always be with us. Jesus tells us that heaven is waiting for us and that our sorrow and pain will be replaced with unspeakable joy. He will wipe every tear from our eyes. There will be no more death or mourning or crying or pain (Revelation 21:4).

A short time ago, following an extended hospital stay, I visited my doctor for a checkup. The walk to his office was long, and I was out of breath when I finally arrived. I knew I could never get up to his office on the third floor without some help.

One of the nurses came and took me up in a wheelchair. I was given a breath test by the nurse when I arrived. She had a hard time taking a reading and told the doctor of her concern. I have COPD and use an oxygen tank at night. But I am able to get through the day with an inhaler that I take in the morning and an emergency inhaler, just in case I need it.

When the doctor examined me, he said that I qualified for oxygen equipment to be used during the day. I was floored. I had several procedures and a surgery several weeks earlier, and I was hoping I would be better by now.

Discouragement flooded my heart, and I left upset. It was late in the afternoon as I drove slowly home. I didn't have any energy and was exhausted most of the time. I felt that God had left.

During the long drive, I happened to look up toward the sky. In amazement, I saw huge, white, puffy clouds that stretched across the heavens. They were in the shape of the cross. The breathtaking sight stayed right in front of me for miles. It was like God was saying, "I have not abandoned you and will always be with you." What a tremendous comfort that was.

Slowly, after one year, I began to feel better. The medications prescribed were changed several times; my diet improved, and I felt stronger. I was able to get out a little and do simple things that delighted my family. I still have a long way to go, but I have hope for the future.

God loves you too, dear friend. Look to Him when you are tired and discouraged. He will never fail to demonstrate His love for you.

God loves you!

Homecoming

No eye has seen, no ear has heard,

no mind has conceived what God has

prepared for those who love him.

—1 Corinthians 2:9

Dearly Beloved,

Many years ago, God gave me a glimpse of heaven. One sunny afternoon in late summer, I was sitting with my prayer partner outside my office under the windmill. We were praying for a dear friend of mine who was going through a difficult time. After the prayer I looked at my prayer partner.

Her face shone with tiny specks of gold, even in her eyelashes! She was the most beautiful creature I had ever seen.

"Oh, Lord," I breathed, "is this what we will look like when we get to heaven?" I knew we would be even more beautiful because we will have brand-new bodies, like our precious Lord Jesus Christ.

> His face was like the sun shining in all its brilliance (Revelation 1:16).

> When he appears, we shall be like him (1 John 3:2).

But our citizenship is in heaven. And we eagerly await a Savior from there, the Lord Jesus Christ, who, by the power that enables him to bring everything under his control, will transform our lowly bodies so that they will be like his glorious body (Philippians 3:20–21).

Can you imagine, dearly beloved? Heaven will be

a place of glorious ecstasy and pure delight. John, the beloved disciple of Christ, described the Holy City, Jerusalem, coming down out of heaven from God. It shone with the glory of God, and its brilliance was like that of a very precious jewel (Revelation 21:10–11).

Many years ago I was in a horrible automobile accident that left my beautiful new car smashed and my body filled with pain for months. In the midst of my suffering, the Lord gave me a preview of heaven.

One Sunday, following a tremendous church service, I was on my way to Beaverdam to visit my daughter. The ride through the countryside was quite beautiful. Sounds and smells of summer were everywhere. Flowers bloomed profusely along the path, cows grazed contentedly in the pasture, and birds were singing in unison as I drove down the country road.

Struck by the magnificent beauty, I began singing praises to God. In adoration and wonder I exclaimed, "Lord, this is what heaven looks like!"

At that moment I rounded a bend in the road. To my utter amazement there were millions of tiny golden butterflies as far as my eyes could see. They were everywhere—in the fields, in the air, in the road. I had to dodge to keep from hitting them. They were beautiful.

It seemed like I drove for miles with those exquisite butterflies flooding the countryside. Then I heard a voice deep inside me say, "Heather, this is what heaven really looks like!"

Dearly beloved, Jesus is preparing a place in heaven just for you! We will see our friends and loved ones, and we will be with our Lord forever. Keep your eyes on Him, and know that He cares for you. For you are His beloved child.

I love you!

Epilogue

The following stories were written by my mother who will turn one hundred years old this year.

Saving the Grasshoppers

> And God said, "Let the land produce living creatures according to their kinds: livestock, creatures that move along the ground, and wild animals, each according to its kind." And it was so, God made the wild animals according to their kinds, the livestock according to their kinds, and all the creatures that move along the ground according to their kinds. And God saw that it was good.

—Genesis 1:24–25

It was a beautiful day in late spring when my mother said, "Heather, go get your bathing suit. I am fixing a picnic lunch, and you and Daddy and I are going to Colonial Beach to spend the day."

So Mother packed a lunch, a peanut butter and jelly sandwich for me (my favorite) and some bananas. Then she got some towels, and we all got into Daddy's car and drove to Colonial Beach. It took one hour and a half.

Colonial Beach, Virginia is beautiful, all-white sand with huge trees and picnic tables with benches scattered around. Daddy picked out a table in the shade, and we unpacked lunch and our bath towels.

Then I ran down to play in the water. That spring there was an invasion of grasshoppers. They came in clouds. The grasshoppers were landing in the water and being washed ashore by the waves. I thought they were drowning and decided to save as many as I could. I found a little stick and started running to the water, picking up as many as I could, and then running back and putting them on the dry sand.

A little boy about my size was at the next table with his mother and dad. He found a little stick and came over to help me. I didn't know his name. We spent the whole day bringing in the grasshoppers. So we always called it "Saving the Grasshoppers Day."

A Gold Star

The King will reply," I tell you the truth,

whatever you did for one of the least of

these brothers of mine, you did for me."

—Matthew 25:40

It was Christmas week, and I was eight years old. Snow had fallen in the night, and the whole world was white and sparkly.

Mother said, "Heather, let's get on the streetcar and go downtown to see Santa Claus." The streetcar was seven cents for Mother; children under twelve rode for free. It was filled with people. Everybody was laughing and talking and having a grand time. Some of the ladies had tiny pieces of mistletoe pinned to their collars.

We were headed for the huge four-story Miller and Rhoads Department store at Broad and Fifth Streets in Richmond, Virginia where a real-live Santa Claus with wavy white hair and a long white beard sat in a big red chair. Nearby, a huge Christmas tree was covered with red, yellow, blue, and green lights. Lines of excited little children waited to climb onto Santa's knee and whisper in his ear what they wanted him to bring them for Christmas. My mother said I was too bashful to get on Santa's knee and would only lean on the arm of his chair.

Outside the line of children, parents were waiting and laughing while they took pictures of their children talking to Santa. As they left Santa's chair, each child was given a handful of little candies by the Christmas elf dressed in green and a cap decorated with tiny bells.

Then all the children held their parents' hands firmly as they walked around the big toy department filled with shiny red bicycles, wagons, and toy tractors.

There were doll carriages packed with beautiful dolls with long golden hair and dressed in pretty dresses and little red coats and hats. There were baby dolls that said, "Momma," when you picked them up and turned them over. Christmas scenes were in every store window. They highlighted scenes from a classic Christmas poem. It was a happy time.

At the corner of Miller and Rhoads stood a five and ten cent store named Woolworth's. Inside the store there were counters filled with tiny dolls, little girls' jewelry, small toys, trucks, and all kinds of Christmas decorations. It was fun walking through the store and looking at all the pretty things.

When we left Woolworth's and went around the corner to get on the streetcar, we saw an old man sitting on a stool with handmade holly Christmas wreaths, strings of running cedar, and small bunches of mistletoe for sale. His big hands were cracked, and some of his fingers were bleeding from making the wreaths. When my mother saw him she said, "Heather, let's go back into Woolworth's for a minute." This time we went down to the basement, where there were men's pants and shirts, cotton socks, and work gloves. I didn't know why we were down there; all the pretty things were upstairs.

Mother went to the pile of gloves and looked through them until she found the biggest pair. She paid for them, and we went back outside and around the corner, where the elderly gentleman was still sitting. Mother gave him the gloves and said, "Merry Christmas." He looked so surprised. Probably no one had ever given him a present and wished him, "Merry Christmas" before.

I exclaimed excitedly, "Mother, you get a good star!" We never saw the old man again, but I hope he felt blessed during that magical Christmas season. I certainly did.

My Prayer Journal

_____

_____

_____

_____

_____

_____

_____

_____

_____

_____

_____

_____

_____

_____

_____

My Prayer Journal

_____

_____

_____

_____

_____

_____

_____

_____

_____

_____

_____

_____

_____

_____

_____

_____

_____

My Prayer Journal

My Prayer Journal

_____

_____

_____

_____

_____

_____

_____

_____

_____

_____

_____

_____

_____

_____

My Prayer Journal

_____

_____

_____

_____

_____

_____

_____

_____

_____

_____

_____

_____

_____

_____

_____

_____

My Prayer Journal

_____

_____

_____

_____

_____

_____

_____

_____

_____

_____

_____

_____

_____

_____

_____

_____

My Prayer Journal

_____

_____

_____

_____

_____

_____

_____

_____

_____

_____

_____

_____

_____

_____

_____

Printed in the United States
By Bookmasters